EDGE
BOOKS

SCARY STORIES

# CREEPY
## URBAN LEGENDS

BY TIM O'SHEI

Consultant:
Simon J. Bronner, PhD
Distinguished Professor of American Studies and Folklore
Fellow, American Folklore Society
The Pennsylvania State University, Harrisburg

CAPSTONE PRESS
a capstone imprint

Edge Books are published by Capstone Press,
151 Good Counsel Drive, P.O. Box 669, Mankato, Minnesota 56002.
www.capstonepub.com

Printed in the United States of America in North Mankato, Minnesota.
032010
005740CGF10

*Library of Congress Cataloging-in-Publication Data*
O'Shei, Tim.
  Creepy urban legends / by Tim O'Shei.
    p. cm.—(Edge books. Scary stories)
  Summary: "Describes scary urban legends, including The Vanishing Hitchhiker
and The Babysitter on the Phone"—Provided by publisher.
  Includes bibliographical references and index.
  ISBN 978-1-4296-4572-0 (library binding)
  1. Urban folklore. 2. Tall tales. 3. Horror tales. I. Title. II. Series.
  GR78.O75 2011
  398.2—dc22                                                      2010001362

**Editorial Credits**
Megan Peterson, editor; Ted Williams, designer; Kelly Garvin, media researcher;
    Laura Manthe, production specialist

**Photo Credits**
Capstone Studio/Karon Dubke, scaremeter, 4, 13, 15, 17, 21, 23, 25, 26, 29
Dreamstime/Artyom Yefimov, 10
Shutterstock/Jacob Hamblin, 8; Kristin Smith, 7; Nick Alexander, cover; Vicki
    France, 18
**Design Elements**
Shutterstock/averole (hand prints), Charles Taylor (rusty background), David
    M. Schrader (paper w/tape), DCD (dribbles), Eugene Ivanov (border), George
    Nazmi Bebawi (fly), Gordan (borders), Hal_P (fingerprints), hfng (word
    bubble), Ian O'Ha (spider web), Kirsty Pargeter (brush strokes border),
    oxygen64 (frames), Ralf Juergen Kraft (computer bug), silver-john (paper),
    Subbotina Anna (fly), Thomas Bethge (tapes), xjbxjhxm123 (button)

# TABLE OF CONTENTS

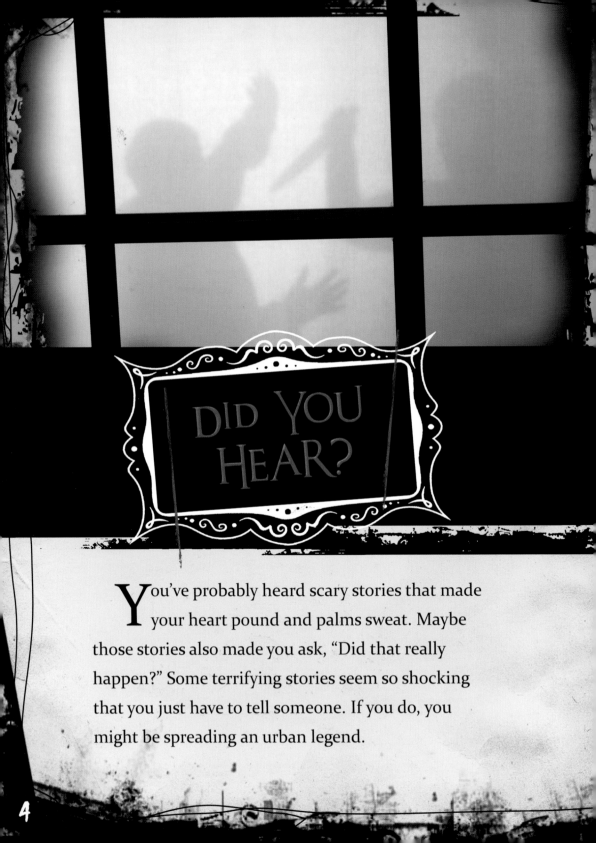

# DID YOU HEAR?

You've probably heard scary stories that made your heart pound and palms sweat. Maybe those stories also made you ask, "Did that really happen?" Some terrifying stories seem so shocking that you just have to tell someone. If you do, you might be spreading an urban legend.

An urban legend is a surprising, often scary story that is told as if it were true. It's usually shared by word of mouth or by e-mail. Most urban legends take place in current times, or in the not-too-distant past. But specific time frames are often left out of the story. Although it might seem unlikely, almost everything that takes place in an urban legend could happen in real life.

Scary urban legends prey upon some of our common fears, such as sleeping in the dark or babysitting at night. Urban legends teach us lessons, often by reminding us what not to do. The stories you're about to read are some of the scariest tales ever told. Lock the doors, and get ready to scream.

## FEAR FACT

"Urban" means relating to a city, but urban legends don't have to take place in a city. They can happen anywhere. The word "urban" is used because it suggests they are tales that could happen today.

# THE DEADLY HAIRDO

SCARY

Lots of people care about what their hair looks like. But some people are fussy enough to do some crazy things to make their hair just right.

In the 1950s, a girl spent many weeks getting ready for her high school's spring dance. A boy she liked would be there, and she wanted to impress him. She bought a new dress and borrowed a pair of high heels from her best friend. The girl's mom took her to a store to buy makeup. But the girl still had to do something about her hair. It was long and stick straight. She decided a **beehive** hairdo would make her stand out.

beehive—a hairstyle that is shaped like a tall cone

The beehive was a popular hairstyle in the 1950s and 1960s.

A month before the dance, the girl washed her hair with sugar water. She pulled her hair up straight, wrapped it in bandages, and lay down carefully in bed. Overnight her hair hardened into a tall, stiff beehive.

Over the next few weeks, the girl refused to wash her hair. She used several cans of hair spray to keep her beehive in place. The girl received many compliments about her new 'do. But she also felt sick and weak. And she began to have terrible headaches. "I must be nervous about the dance," the girl thought.

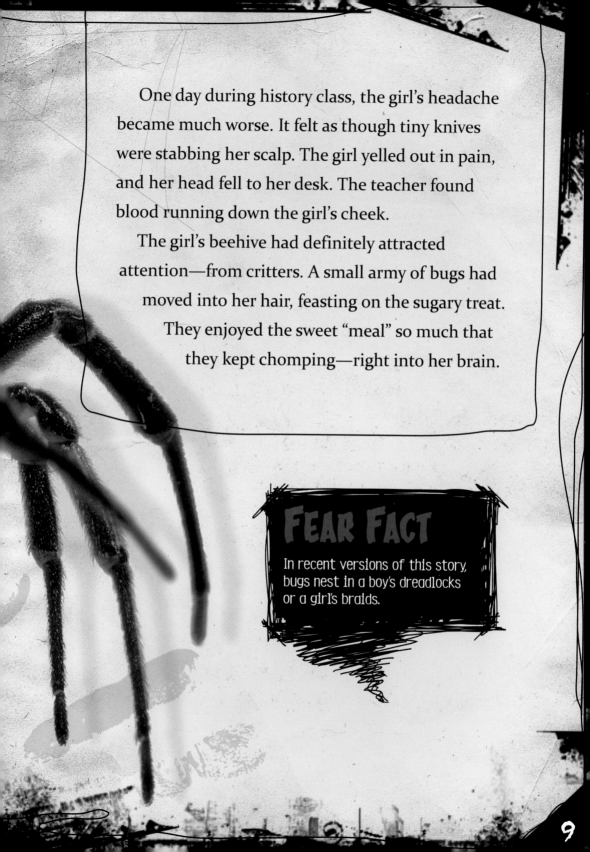

One day during history class, the girl's headache became much worse. It felt as though tiny knives were stabbing her scalp. The girl yelled out in pain, and her head fell to her desk. The teacher found blood running down the girl's cheek.

The girl's beehive had definitely attracted attention—from critters. A small army of bugs had moved into her hair, feasting on the sugary treat. They enjoyed the sweet "meal" so much that they kept chomping—right into her brain.

## FEAR FACT

In recent versions of this story, bugs nest in a boy's dreadlocks or a girl's braids.

# DON'T TURN ON THE LIGHT

VERY SCARY

Two college roommates didn't have much in common. One liked to hang out with her friends. The other liked to study.

One night, the more outgoing girl asked her roommate to go bowling. But the roommate declined. She had to prepare for a science test. The first girl also needed to study. But she planned on doing it when she got back. Besides, bowling with friends might help her relax.

It was late when the girl returned from bowling. The lights in the dorm room were out. The girl could see the dark shape of her roommate asleep in bed. She decided not to turn on the light. Instead, she would wake up early to study. She might even ask her roommate for help.

But the girl had a hard time sleeping that night. She kept hearing faint noises, but she couldn't make out what they were. A rolling sound and then a pounding sound kept her awake. "The noises from the bowling alley must be stuck in my head," she thought.

Morning arrived, and sunlight flooded the room. The girl woke up, rubbed her eyes, and started to focus on her roommate's side of the room. She really hoped her friend would help her study.

But the roommate couldn't help her study—not today, and not ever. The roommate was dead. Written in blood on the ceiling were the words, "Aren't you glad you didn't turn on the light?"

## FEAR FACT

Versions of this story were first collected in the 1960s. In one version, the roommate who stays in for the night survives. She hears banging and scratching sounds in the hallway. Terrified, the girl locks the door. The next morning, she discovers her roommate's bloody body in the hallway.

Aren't you glad you didn't turn on the light?

# THE BABYSITTER ON THE PHONE

**VERY SCARY**

On a dark night, a 15-year-old girl was babysitting three kids. It was a quiet job—all the kids were asleep upstairs. The babysitter turned off the lights and settled on the couch to watch TV. Through the window she could see a full moon. Other than the chatter of the TV, the only sound was the wind whipping through the trees outside.

The house phone rang.

At first startled by the sudden noise, the babysitter quickly calmed down. It was just a phone call. "Hello?" she asked.

"I've got the kids," croaked a deep voice.

"It's just a prank call," the babysitter thought. "It's probably one of my friends trying to scare me." She hung up the phone. When it rang a few minutes later, the girl thought it might be the children's parents. She answered the call.

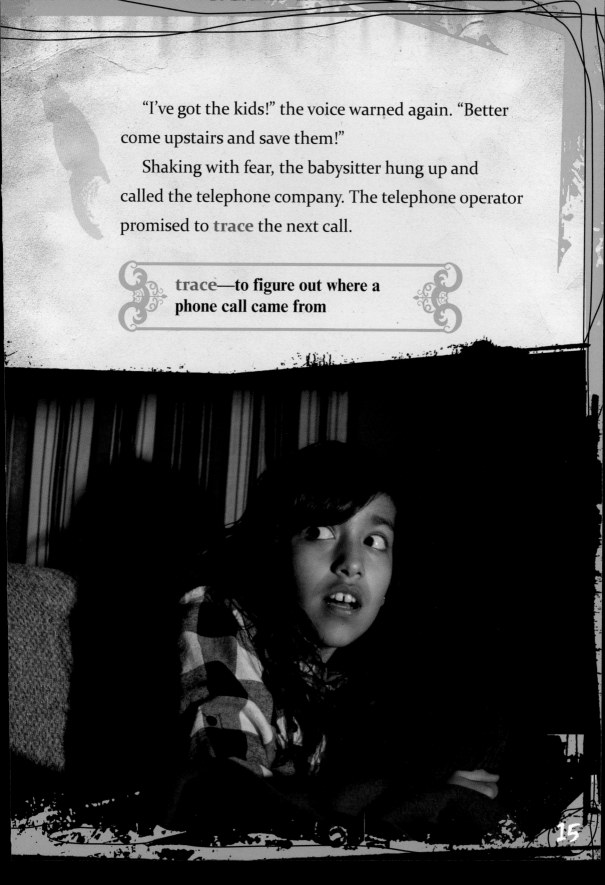

"I've got the kids!" the voice warned again. "Better come upstairs and save them!"

Shaking with fear, the babysitter hung up and called the telephone company. The telephone operator promised to **trace** the next call.

**trace**—to figure out where a phone call came from

The phone rang a third time. With an unsteady hand, the babysitter picked up the phone. "Hello?" she asked, her voice no louder than a whisper.

"Don't hang up on me!" the voice spat. "I've got the kids. And this is your last chance to save them!" Before the girl could utter a word, the caller hung up.

After that third call, the operator called the babysitter. "We can't trace the call," the operator said. "It must be coming from an extension inside the house. Get out now!"

"What about the children?" the babysitter cried. She looked back at the darkened staircase.

"Get out!" the operator repeated. "I've already called the police."

The babysitter ran outside and into the dark front yard. The wind howled around her. Suddenly a dark shape appeared in the moonlight. The girl tried to get away, but a man grabbed her and waved a knife in her face.

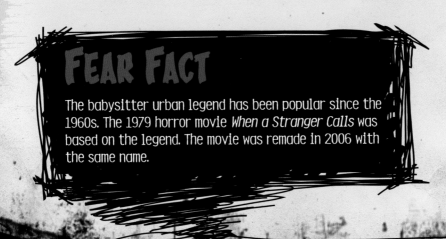

## FEAR FACT

The babysitter urban legend has been popular since the 1960s. The 1979 horror movie *When a Stranger Calls* was based on the legend. The movie was remade in 2006 with the same name.

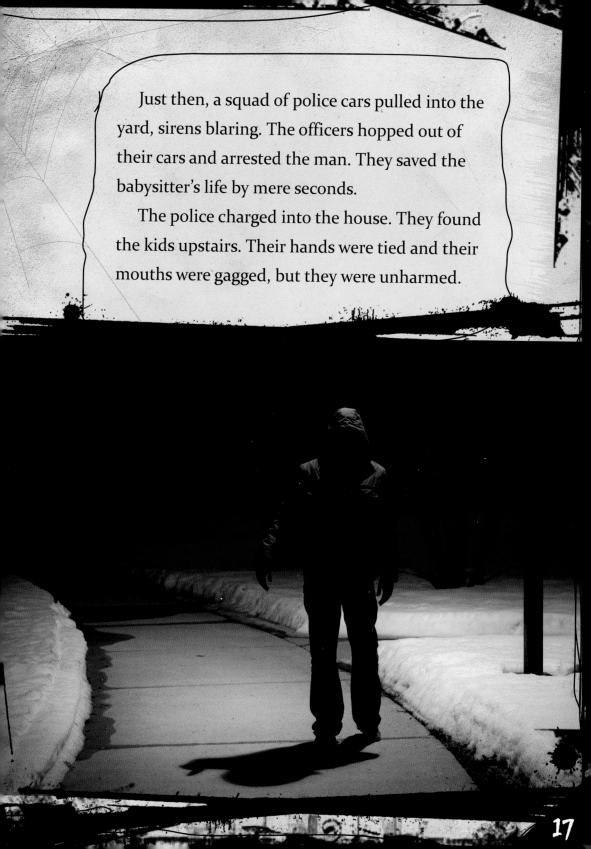

Just then, a squad of police cars pulled into the yard, sirens blaring. The officers hopped out of their cars and arrested the man. They saved the babysitter's life by mere seconds.

The police charged into the house. They found the kids upstairs. Their hands were tied and their mouths were gagged, but they were unharmed.

# THE SWINGING MAN

Running out of gas during the day is annoying. Running out of gas in the dark is scary. Running out of gas in the dark in the middle of nowhere is terrifying.

That's what happened one night to a boyfriend and girlfriend. They were driving on a quiet, unlit country road when the car ran out of gas. Thick woods lined both sides of the road. No houses were within sight.

The car rolled to a stop beneath a tree. The boyfriend told his girlfriend he was going to walk into town for help. He asked her to lock the doors and stay inside no matter what. The girlfriend agreed. The boyfriend walked toward the road and was soon swallowed up by the darkness.

With little to do but wait, the girlfriend tried to get some sleep. But a soft scratching sound on the top of the car kept her awake. The girlfriend decided a low-hanging tree branch must be hitting the car. She wanted to step out and swipe the branch away, but she had promised not to open the door. The girlfriend tried to pass the time by listening to the radio. She twisted the dial but could only get static. She listened carefully for the sound of passing cars. "Maybe if someone drives by," she thought, "I'll get out and ask for help." But the road remained vacant. The only sound was the scritch-scratch of the branch on the car's roof.

Finally, the girlfriend curled up beneath her jacket and fell asleep. She awoke in the morning to the sound of sirens. Suddenly something tapped against the window. The girl jumped, but it was only a police officer. Confused and scared, she opened the door and asked what was happening. The officer led her away from the car. He told her not to look back.

But the girlfriend didn't listen to the police officer. She looked back and saw the source of the scratching. It was her boyfriend, dead, hanging upside down from the tree! His arm was dangling down, and his fingernails were scraping the top of the car. Scritch-scratch.

# THE VANISHING HITCHHIKER

FREAKY SCARY

The night was quiet and lonely, and the salesman was tired. He had spent the day selling vacuums door-to-door. Now he was driving on a long, dark highway, heading to the next town.

Suddenly, in the darkness, he saw a young woman standing on the side of the road. She held her arm out and her thumb up. She was a hitchhiker. The salesman stopped the car and rolled down the window.

"Could you give me a ride to the next town?" the woman asked. "I live there with my parents."

The man paused. Picking up hitchhikers is never a good idea. But this woman seemed so tired and cold. Her cheeks were pale, and she pulled her thin sweatshirt tightly around her chest.

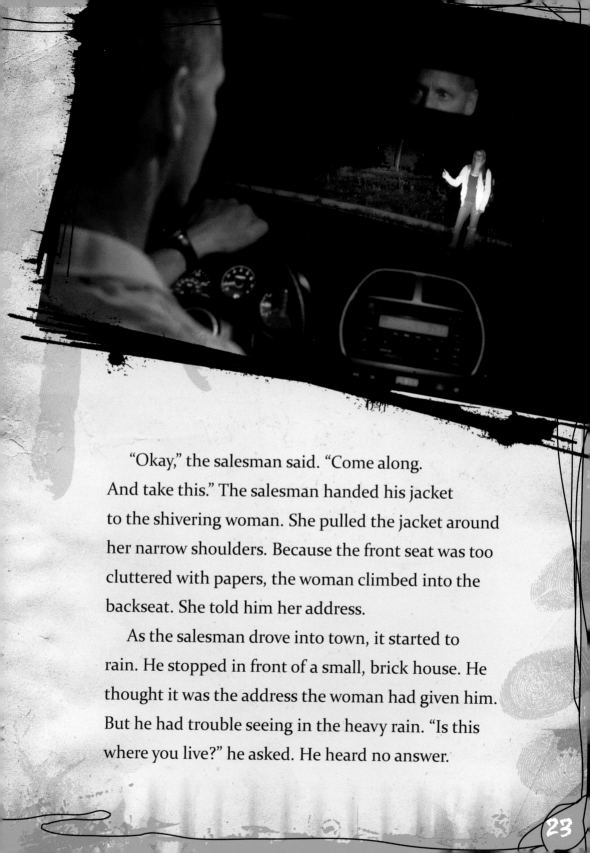

"Okay," the salesman said. "Come along.
And take this." The salesman handed his jacket
to the shivering woman. She pulled the jacket around
her narrow shoulders. Because the front seat was too
cluttered with papers, the woman climbed into the
backseat. She told him her address.

As the salesman drove into town, it started to
rain. He stopped in front of a small, brick house. He
thought it was the address the woman had given him.
But he had trouble seeing in the heavy rain. "Is this
where you live?" he asked. He heard no answer.

"It's late, and she must be tired," the salesman thought. "Maybe she didn't hear me." He repeated the question but got no response.

Could the woman have fallen asleep? The salesman turned around and got his answer. She was gone! There was no sign of the hitchhiker. Even the salesman's coat had vanished.

The next morning, the salesman drove back to the address the woman had given him. He knocked on the front door, and a woman answered. She looked like the hitchhiker but much older. "This must be her mother," he thought.

The salesman explained to the woman that he had tried to give her daughter a ride home. The woman ran back into the house.

Then a man with hunched shoulders and dark circles under his eyes came to the door. He was holding a wrinkled photograph.

The salesman pointed to the photo. "That's the woman I gave a ride to," he said.

The man shook his head. "Our daughter has been dead for many years."

The salesman followed the man to a nearby cemetery. The man pointed to a gravestone. "This is where our daughter is buried," he said. On top of the grave lay the salesman's missing coat!

## FEAR FACT

The story of the vanishing hitchhiker is one of the oldest and most widespread urban legends. In older versions of the tale, the vehicle is a buggy pulled by horses.

FACT OR
FICTION?

Are urban legends true? Not word-for-word. Every urban legend changes over time. Storytellers like to add to or **exaggerate** a story's details. The changes can be small. Sometimes the vanishing hitchhiker leaves behind a book or purse. The driver gives the object to the girl's family. The changes can also be big. For instance, the babysitter urban legend sometimes ends with the police finding the children dead. And sometimes there isn't a killer at all—it's the children playing a prank on their babysitter.

Still, these stories could be based on real-life events. People driving in the middle of the night sometimes see strangers hitchhiking on the side of the road. Cars do run out of gas. And who hasn't been scared by a late-night phone call while babysitting?

**exaggerate**—to make something seem bigger, better, or more important than it really is

The stories in this book might be close to the truth. We'll never know for certain, but maybe that's better. Guessing whether or not an urban legend is true can be more fun than knowing for sure!

# PERFECT YOUR SCARY STORYTELLING

To tell a truly creepy urban legend, start by saying something like, "This happened to a friend of a friend." Add details like names, places, time of day, and what the weather was like. Is it dark outside? Does your tale take place in the middle of a thunderstorm? A howling blizzard? Be sure to keep your audience in suspense. Hint at what might happen, but don't give it away until the very end. Imagine scary music playing as you tell your story. Better yet, play scary music as you tell your tale.

# GLOSSARY

**beehive** (BEE-hive)—a hairstyle that is shaped like a tall cone

**exaggerate** (eg-ZAJ-uh-rate)—to make something seem bigger, better, or more important than it really is

**extension** (ek-STEN-shun)—an extra telephone line connected to the main line

**gag** (GAYG)—to put a gag on someone; a gag is a piece of cloth put in or over someone's mouth to keep them from speaking or screaming

**hitchhiker** (HICH-hiker)—a person who travels by getting rides in other people's vehicles

**trace** (TRAYSS)—to figure out where a phone call came from

**vacant** (VAY-kuhnt)—empty or not occupied

# READ MORE

**Axelrod-Contrada, Joan.** *Ghoulish Ghost Stories.* Scary Stories. Mankato, Minn.: Capstone Press, 2011.

**Kallen, Stuart A.** *Urban Legends.* The Mystery Library. Farmington Hills, Mich.: Lucent Books, 2006.

**Lynette, Rachel.** *Urban Legends.* Mysterious Encounters. Detroit: KidHaven Press, 2008.

**Olson, Arielle North, and Howard Schwartz.** *More Bones: Scary Stories from around the World.* New York: Viking, 2008.

# INTERNET SITES

FactHound offers a safe, fun way to find Internet sites related to this book. All of the sites on FactHound have been researched by our staff.

Here's all you do:

Visit *www.facthound.com*

Type in this code: 9781429645720

# INDEX